Chrysalis

❀ ❀ ❀

Not Quite The Butterfly

Ikea Williams

Copyright © 2016 by Ikea Williams

All rights reserved. No part of this book may be reproduced in any form by any electronic or mechanical means including photocopying, recording, or information storage and retrieval without permission in writing from the author.

Table of Contents

1	WORDS OF WISDOM
3	MY SILVER SPOON
5	HOME RUN
7	FLY AWAY
9	A CHILD'S ASPIRATION
12	MY IMAGINARY FRIEND
14	CUSTODY
17	SILENT WAR
20	THE KEY
21	THE VOLUME OF MY HAIR
26	POTS AND KETTLES
27	THAT'S WHAT "THEY" TOLD ME
29	MEAN GREEN
31	WAKING UP
32	SORRY IF I'M TOO GAY FOR YOU TODAY
35	DINOSAURS
39	DIY
43	NOT THE FURNITURE STORE
46	BLACK ANGEL
49	2 P'S NO POD
52	RED SHARPIE
55	POPPED CHERRY
58	ODE TO MY CITY

Dedication

To Great-Grandma, Uncle Paul and Aunt Dorothy for playing an integral role in my early childhood development and continuing to watch over me

To Nana for your love and your immaculate strength and for keeping it together

To Auntie Tonya for loving me like a daughter and your continual sacrifice and selflessness

To my Mother, Pauline, for the fighter and survivor in you and passing the gene along to me

To my sisters, Jazmine, Candace and Breanna for making me tough and showing me how to navigate this world

To my mentor, friend, mother figure and Guardian Angel on earth Ta-Shana Taylor for recognizing my potential from day one and keeping me on the path of success

To my sister/cousin Jamila for being my other half and always supporting my decisions no matter what

Foreword

Growing up, I've always felt misunderstood. As I got older I realized why. I was never big on explaining myself and it wasn't because I didn't want to, but because I didn't know how, not out loud at least. Writing has always been a strength of mine and when all else fails, I can always depend on written words. So here, in my poetic autobiography, are all the things I couldn't say out loud.

Words of Wisdom

She glided, floated almost, as she entered the room
I sat and stared in awe, too afraid to move
My eyes fixed on her hair that illuminated like the sun
We embraced for what seemed like eternity
I inhaled her scent, the one that was burned into my memory
We let go reluctantly
Took our seats
Began our feast
Jelly and crackers cuz that was our favorite
Popcorn and Welch's grape soda was our sunshine on the rainy days
How I wish it was still that easy
I broke the silence with "Why did you leave me?"
She replied "You no longer needed me".
I said, "You were gone when I needed you most"
"My absence was the greater presence.
You've made it through your adolescence
As you have yet to learn a lifetime of lessons.
If you're asking me why I let go of your hand, I'm sure one day you'll understand".
Her voice was as calming as a sea breeze
We talked some more as I let that sink in
And soon our dinner had come to an end
I got up from the table to escort her to the door
We embraced for what seemed like eternity once more
"If ever you feel I'm too far, just close your eyes and I'll be in your dreams"

I smiled and said "I love you"
As I handed her a halo and Angel wings

-*For Grandma*

My Silver Spoon

1992, Born with a silver spoon in my mouth
1997, God came and took it out
Ever since then
Life's been plastic cups
And paper plates
Got a bone to pick
With that man at the golden gates
You see, I could never comprehend
Why he took my silver spoon
Outshone the sun, stars and moon
It was the exclusive edition
The one not sold in stores
Singled out from all the other
Utensils in the draw
I treated that spoon
With intensive care
Acknowledged you for
Always being there
My silver spoon
Made eating look lavish
I boasted because
No one else could have it
Now it's gone
I never asked for you to hand me
The world on a silver platter

Without my silver spoon
It doesn't even matter
But I'll get you back
I'll see you soon
I'll be on the cows back
When he jumps over the moon

Home Run

First base

Was the first place I called home

The place of middle of the night cries to be held

Or changed

Or fed

The place of bike rides, scraped knees and busted lips

The place of cousins on the weekend, cartoons and bowls of cereal

The place of runny noses and Vick's vapor rub on the chest

Wide tooth combs, plats and barrettes

It's a place I'll never forget

Second base was the second place

Sort of like first base, except there was less space

This place was fried chicken you could smell from half a block away

Walking home from school

The sound of Court T.V. all day, Jeopardy at 7 and Wheel of Fortune at 7:30

The sound of scary movies on the couch with my sisters eating homemade popcorn

The sound of Sega Genesis and Nintendo 64 and Kangol hats on the walls

The reenactment of all of Aaliyah's videos

And the sound of Donnell Jones "Where I Wanna be" blasting from the radio with the foil covered antenna

The smell of Hot combs on the stove top and Dax grease

The sound of backyard cookouts and neighbors bringing dishes and making to go plates

The feeling of catching fireflies in plastic cups, covering it with foil and poked holes in it for air
The taste of nacho cheese sunflower seeds from the store across the street and quarter waters in every flavor
These are the days that I tried to savor
But I had no say in the matter
As we were then placed at third base
The place of some of the coldest winter's ever
But some of the best summer's
Like playing double-dutch out front with the neighbors from next door
Or middle of the night store runs for a bacon, egg and cheese on a roll
Kit Kat's and cheese doodles
Visits to the local library was the hang out spot
Or the park across the street from it where my sisters' played basketball
The place of Barbie dolls until 3 a.m. and the same pajamas all weekend
The place of broken curfews and teenage parties
A little underage drinking just to see what the fuss was all about
The place of walking around the block several times for no reason
It seemed we had a new home every season
There's no place like home
So I clicked my heels 3 times to try to get back
But there was no home to get back to
Only the memories I've been chasing
Trynna find my way back to first base
Should've never left in the first place
But I was too young to decide on my own
I would've chose 3 strikes if that meant never leaving home

Fly Away

I want to spread my wings and fly
Never to return
I want to fly close to the sun
And let it burn
I want to fly to the other end of the world
And see all there is to see
I want to be able to fly freely
And be me
I want to fly with the eagles, pigeon and swans
I want to fly over the Amazon
I want to fly across the Atlantic Ocean
And the Caribbean Sea
I want to fly to Atlanta
And Kentucky
I want to fly high to the sky
And meet the moon and stars
I want to go to Pluto
I want to go to Mars
I want to fly to China
I want to fly to Spain
I want to fly with all the airplanes
I want to fly to Miami
I want to fly to Jamaica
I want to fly to Europe
And even Africa

I want to fly away because I'm no longer caged
I want to fly away before I reach my dying age
I want to fly and see what's in store
I want to see all the beauty of the world before it gets destroyed

A Child's Aspiration

When I was 11
My 6th grade teacher asked the class
"What do you want to be when you grow up?"
I sat quietly to the back of the class
As I listened to my classmates robotically spew the basic responses
"Doctor, lawyer, firefighter, teacher."
She slowly made her way around the room
And soon
It was my turn
"And Ikea, what about you?
What do you want to be when you get older?"
I paused for a moment before answering,
"A crack pipe"
The room filled with "Huh's" and "What" and even a few chuckles
I saw the confusion and concern in my teacher's eyes
As she saw the seriousness in mine
I spared her the embarrassment of having to ask why
And replied
"I always wondered what it would feel like to be held by my mother"
To be held on to for dear life
To feel like if you ever let me go you'd die
I want you to inhale me so deeply your lungs could collapse
I want to be what makes you feel like nothing else in this world matters
Because I make you so high you can't see or think about anything but me
I want you to spend your last crumpled up dollar

That you found in your raggedy pants pocket
Just to make sure I'm filled
I want you to do something strange for some change
Because you gotta have me and can't go another minute without me
I want you to go through withdrawals
From being away from me for so long
And waste no time getting me back in your grasp when we reunite
I want to be the reason you go days,
Even weeks
Without passing a comb through your hair
Or a wash rag to your body
Because hygiene isn't a priority
When your only concern is me
I want you to look into the eyes of strangers
And lie
And beg and plead
To fulfill that need
To feed me
I want you to walk up and down the street
Sun up till sundown
Asking around for some spare change
And when you got enough
You spend it all on me
The lips that were supposed to
Kiss my forehead at night
Tell me to sleep tight
And don't let the bed bugs bite
Was pressed against the tip
Of a crack pipe
I want to be
What makes your world filled with no worries
However brief

I want you to sacrifice
Lose your sense of being
Sense of pride
Sense
All because I make you feel good inside
I want you to keep trying
To relive the moment you first saw me
When your curiosity was piqued
And you had no idea
The power I held
But you knew in that moment
You had to try
Pick me up
Hold me
Handle me with care in fear that you might break me
Take a deep breath
Sigh
And prepare for me to change your life
I want to know what it is
About that bond
Between that crack and that pipe
That would make you devote your life to it
And abandon the one you created
So simply put, teacher
I just want to be loved

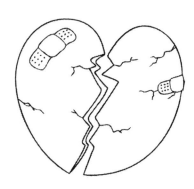

My Imaginary Friend

You told me you loved me
You said you'd never leave me
Damn
There I go again make-believing
I used to play pretend
With my Imaginary friend
You know, you make one of those
So you don't have to feel alone
We imagined up all the things I never had
One that was frequent was a mom and dad
But my Imaginary friend couldn't hug me
My Imaginary friend couldn't love me
My Imaginary friend
Couldn't teach me wrong from right
My Imaginary friend
Couldn't teach me how to ride a bike
My Imaginary friend couldn't tie my shoes
But my Imaginary friend knew
My favorite color was Blue
Did you?
My Imaginary friend knows my biggest fears
My Imaginary friend saw the pain in my tears
My Imaginary friend gave a listening ear
While I told him all the things
I wanted to hear

Like you telling me you love me
Saying you'd never leave me
But I got so damn tired
Of make-believing
They say what don't kill you
Makes you stronger
I'm too strong
To make believe any longer

Custody

Every night I lose sleep
Lying awake
Listening to a child weep
Knees to chest
Chin to knees
Wiping tears with her sleeves
Back and forth she rocks
As I plead with her to stop
For this has gone on for years
I can't tolerate one more tear
She says the tears are not her own
She just doesn't like to be alone
I said, "I understand how much company misery needs
But choose some other company to keep"
She said, "I'm not the misery, I am the company"
"You see, I wish there was somewhere else to go
I don't want to be the one
Who keeps you up at night
While you wish me away
But I can't leave until you confront me
You thought you left me behind
But you haven't gone very far
I'm right on your heels
To remind you that we've got things to discuss
Things you refuse to confront

Like your fear that someday soon you'll be gone
Without leaving a worthy mark
Things like all the risks you didn't take
And all the excuses you continue to make
You spend more time dreaming about living
Than living your dreams
That's why you have trouble
Falling asleep
So don't pick a fight with me
Because you're not who you said
You'd grow up to be
You are not living your truth
And I'm simply the messenger
So please don't shoot"
As much as I wanted to put up a fight
I couldn't deny that the child was right
I've been trying to let go of
What I should be holding on to
I keep getting redirected
To the place I belong to
My inner child has been waiting
For me to come out and play
No matter rain or shine
She just won't go away
So I decided
To go ahead and give in
I had to pick my battles
And this one I wouldn't win
I said "Ok, Ok!"
Then she grabbed my hand
She smiled at me
As I let her lead the way

We played dress up
And make believe
Reversed all of the lies
Life made me believe
Like "The dreams of a child
Eventually die"
But the dream and the child
Are both still alive
The child only grows older
And may get jaded
But my vision is clear
And my dreams aren't faded
So I'll do away
With all I've been told
Because inhibitions
Never help you grow
So they'll be no more tears
No keeping me up at night
We both went to sleep
And had the rest of our lives

Silent War

I wish that you could hear the noise inside my head
The noise that keeps me up at night as I lie in my bed
Trying to silence it
Is as difficult as hushing an auditorium filled with 1st graders
But even they settle down eventually
There are many different voices
The loudest is the one that tells me
That sleep is the remedy
I love sleep and wish to do it all the time
Sleep, forever
And then I realize
How much that sounds like death
My doctor says I'm depressed
Maybe even a hint of bipolar
we wont diagnose you just yet
But we'll leave it on the table
I never did well with labels
When I die I'll be put in a box
So I refuse to live in one
I am not depressed
I am merely weathering the storm
Actually a few storms
Maybe even a few tornadoes
Throw in an occasional hurricane
And sometimes my earth quakes

And sometimes my heart aches
But I will not be another test subject for the latest
Anti depressant
That turns humans
Into zombies
So that we may be killed first
if ever there was an apocalypse
I will not push a pill through these lips
I will not be the FDA's Hooray
I will not use a stronger grip on this crutch
I will claw my way out of the darkness
Like a cat trying to get out of the house
I will only depend on sleep for the replenishment of my body
For Christ's sake, amen
I will cry because I am releasing demons
Not because I am showing weakness
But because I am winning this fight
And intend on winning the war
I will hurt no more
Not myself
Not those I hurt because they were hurt
To see me see them see me hurt
I will not succumb to this man made
Self proclaimed hell
I will expose my wounds and where them well
This is a single bed
There's no space for you here
Not day or night
I'll tuck myself in
And wish me goodnight
Then replay it all tomorrow in my head

Until I'm counting the fatalities
And not you instead

The Key

It's cuz she's light skinned
Closer to white skin
Than my skin
The right skin
To be in
To win

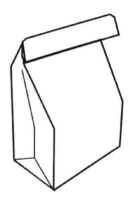

The Volume of My Hair

I would say
That it's just hair and
That I don't really care
But that's not the truth
It's gonna get deep
So let's start from the roots
You see
It started when I was nine
Maybe even ten
But even back then
I couldn't pretend
That my hair was just "fine"
Hot combs on the stove top
Could only put
A temporary stop
To the peas cooking in this pot
So of course
I was forced
To go the course
Of being the lab rat
Of the creamy crack
Just so my ends
Could touch my back
Each month
Perms took turns

Letting my scalp
Feel the burn
Just for looks of approval
In return
But soon I would learn
That I took the wrong turn
Year after year
I watched my hair disappear
And the follicles of my pride
Combed at me inside
But I brushed it off
Chalked it up to a loss
And had little pep talks
Like
"Having naps in the back
Is just part of being black
It's just hair, it will grow back"
And then I made friends
With baseball caps
Fitted to the front
Or twist it to the back
Beanies, hoodies
And snap backs
Can't recall a time
I didn't wear a hat
I let the Brim
Play a Role
I put a cap on my soul
But the hole from within
Had all the control
Some words
That I heard

Still have a hold
Beauty is in the eyes
Of the one who beholds
But that's not what
I was told
Being pretty meant being light
"You'd be pretty
If you were light"
Wasn't something
I took pretty light
Every day was a fight
But I was brave
I made a trade
With my braids
For a Caesar
And got Questions
For my dressing
But I kept them guessing
Cuz there were bigger demons
That I was wrestling
Dark-skinned
No Hair
On top of that I'm Gay
Now I have to deal with
What the world has to say
Got more to worry 'bout
Than what I'm gonna wear today
Trying to solve a problem
Got me running in to more
Went from an inner battle
To a full on war
Wish I could go back

To the way it was before
Not to the naps
But back to when
Blacks were proud
To be just that
Black
When Afro Picks
And raised fists
Was the shit!
Before Madame CJ Walker
Convinced us to conform
To "social norms"
Back to when
We let our soul glow
It seems
We let our souls go
Back to when grandma
Palmed your face
And looked in your eyes
And said baby you are beautiful
Don't let anyone tell you otherwise
Or when momma stood you in front of the mirror
And said "love what you see
The mirror is reflecting you
And you
Are a reflection of me"
Now our reflections
Are on T.V.
Camouflaged in makeup
Covered in weaves
I don't really see
What self love really means

So I would say that
It's just hair
And that I don't really care
But that's not the truth
The truth is
We need to get back
To our roots

Pots and Kettles

Lately I've been rejecting
The things I don't like
In people I see
Carefully picking them apart
As I identify these things
As pieces of me
Then I feel guilty
As I strut around
Clad in my armor
Of hypocrisy
In this state of mind
In this state of mine
I fit in just fine
Content
With this perception
Of a violent-less crime

That's What "They" Told Me

They told me
Life is hard
You have to work for what you want
Nobody is gonna hand anything to you
Go to school
Get your education
Get more education
Get more money
It will all pay off
Because you'll get more money
Lose sleep
Lose weight
Lose my mind
It's OK
You gotta "do what you gotta do"
You'll be alright
You'll be OK
Walk this way
Talk this way
Dress this way
Breathe this way
Blink this way
If you're this way
You'll get far in life
Because

If you're this way
You'll get more money
They told me
Life is hard
You can be whatever you want to be

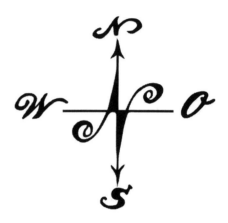

Mean Green

I am the devil in disguise
I am the ultimate prize
I make you kill for me
Die for me
Steal for me
Cry for me
Go to war for me
On all fours for me
Run for me
Hold guns for me
Betray for me
Break day for me
Hurt for me
Work for me
Kneel in the dirt for me
Fight for me
Change your life for me
Lose religion for me
Go to prison for me
Suck for me
Fuck for me
Protect for me
Lose self respect for me
I'll make you needy for me
Greedy for me

Weep for me

Lose sleep for me

Pretend for me

Lose friends for me

Grind for me

Lose your mind for me

Change for me

Do something strange for me

Spread hate for me

Lose weight for me

Spread lies for me

Create a divide for me

Oppress for me

Cause stress for me

Gain control for me

Sell your soul for me

I'll make you love

Put no one above me

Not even God himself

I am the definition of wealth

And my green faces

Can take you many places

Wherever you envision

But these are the terms and conditions

Waking Up

Somehow

I've got a new pair of eyes

And I'm slowly dying inside

I can feel my soul withering away

As it cries out for a savior

My mind has grasped the concept

My heart doesn't want to endure it

My feet don't move

Because they have lost

All sense of direction

But have not lost the sense

To direct

My brain

Is at war with the concept of life

With what everyone

Has been trained to feel

And think

And agree with

And Oppose

And made to believe sensible

When in reality

No one understands

The more different we try to be

The more alike we've become

Sorry if I'm Too Gay for You Today

Sorry if I'm too gay for you today
That I chose this hairstyle
And I'm dressed this way
Sorry if my jeans
Aren't skin tight
And my cleavage isn't
In plain sight
Sorry if I got
Some swag in my walk
A swing in my arm
And some base when I talk
Sorry if my shape up
Is straighter that yours
And my pointed side burns
More faded than yours
Sorry if my chick
Is badder than yours
Hair real, nails real
Ass fatter than yours
Sorry if I don't
Cross my legs when I sit
And don't wear skirts
And heels n shit

Sorry if my girl and I
Are holding hands
And frown at stupid questions like
"Which one is the man?"
Sorry if us kissing
Makes you squirm
Sorry we don't need to fuck you
To use your sperm
Sorry that we still
Have to fight for our rights
And get real defensive
When you call us dykes
Sorry if I never
Gave you the time of day
To make me "change my mind"
About being gay
Sorry if I choose
Not to listen
To your played out speech
Bout "You don't know what you're missing"
Sorry that I love women
Because they're softer
Mentally stronger
And Have more to offer
Sorry that more women
Are jumping on our boat
Maybe you should sit back
Relax and take notes
Sorry if I
Just want equality
To love freely
With no apology

Sorry if my way of loving
Is a sin
And you only see the surface
And not what's within
I'm sorry that
You were born straight
And that your way of living
Doesn't encourage me to hate
I'm sorry that I
Was born this way
And that's not gonna change
No matter how hard you pray
Sorry if I want kids
Because I still can
Just because I'm gay
Doesn't make me a man
Sorry that two mommies
Doesn't seem real
But it's a two parent home
Isn't that ideal?
I'm sorry that my happiness
Isn't up for debate
I'm sorry that you're privileged
And you can't relate
I'm sorry you think
That I should go to hell
I got some buddy passes
You can go as well
I'm sorry but
I'm just keeping it real
Sorry that I really
Don't give a fuck how you feel

Dinosaurs

I woke up feeling a dinosaur

Not because I'm a carnivore or an herbivore

But because I've seen this scene before

Systematic murder galore

I've watched my brothers gunned down

Just because they were brown

I remember hearing Shawn yell

Does that even ring a bell?

They x'd Malcolm off the scene,

Beat down Rodney king

Right on my T.V. screen

And like Martin, told me I was having a dream

Police brutality

Isn't a new reality

It's a rerun marathon

As they pass their baton

Across the backs

Of blacks

And then wonder what's wrong

And why we give them no respect

They neglect their mission

To Serve and protect

But what protection do we get?

It's really hard to detect

Or make any distinction

But like tyrannosaurus Rex
We are up next
To be the victims
Of extinction
This era feels so Jurassic
And what's even more tragic
Is that our lack of unity
Will let them have it
I'm dangling on the edge of hope
The ever so familiar feeling
Of dangling
From the end
Of a rope
Except this time they'll say it was suicide
Anything to try and hide
How she really died
I swallowed my pain for Sandra
But the taste was kind of bland
I battled indigestion
Because I couldn't stomach
Or understand
How the terms of our existence
Is still in their hands
Hands
That dragged us from our mothers
And our lands
Dragged us from the motherland
To a land
Where our mothers
Are burying our brothers
Like well kept secrets
Their pain

Is the deepest
Like the roots
To which we must get back
Otherwise
The history books will write
Once upon a time
There was a species called blacks
They once roamed the earth
They were darker than you and I
Some could swim
And some could fly
But they became endangered
So they all had to die
So we stood our ground
For the sake of our survival
And emptied the clips
Of our .45 calibers, AR 15's
And other Rifles
And the laws we wrote
Made us rightful
No matter how loud we riot
They never get indicted
There's no justice
There's just us
And although we've never seen him
In god we trust
We can March
April, May, and June
But to them
We are still coons
And if we don't stand up
We'll all

be lying
down
soon

Diy

I come from a long line

Of strong women

Who are stronger than

Strong men

Women who have

Lifted weights in their wombs,

Brought them up

And carry them on their shoulders

Women stronger than boulders

Women who

You can believe have conceived on their own

They're so good at doing it alone

We wear independence

Like a badge of honor

Because we have been at war indeed

We wear our purple hearts on our sleeves

Because they've been ripped out of our chests

The same place

Where you can now find a capital "S"

The same place

Nestled between breasts

The breasts that feed the seeds

That will carry on our legacy

I never learned how to ask for help

All I know is "Do it yourself"

As long as you are willing and able
You are more than capable
And if ever you're on your hands and knees
Let it not be to beg
Or to please
But because you are working hard
To provide your own needs
It's words like these
Spoken by my mother's mother
That just makes me wonder
What women are made of
I'm not talking about
Chromosomes and estrogen
I'm talking about
How we manage to sustain hurricanes
With our feet planted firmly in the mud
How we transform crumbs
And bake bread
How we balance the crowns on our heads
While walking on eggshells
Or how we carry burdens
While walking in 6 inch stilettos,
An outfit to match and a clutch
You wouldn't be able to tell
That our day was rough
We made struggle a fashion trend
No need for help
When you wear it so well
I remember
There was this woman
Who didn't wait for a man to take initiative
Because he'd done so

Many times before
Except they called him "massa"
So she got up in the middle of the night
To let her people go
And made several trips without getting caught
Nicknamed "Moses"
A name belonging to a man
Proving that anything he can do,
She can
So I need to understand
What women are made of
Not sugar and spice and everything nice
But she'll take those same ingredients
And make you a well balanced meal,
Put all 5 kids to sleep,
Tie on that satin head scarf
And break day mastering her degrees
Because pursuing an eligible bachelor
Isn't enough to keep a roof over their heads
And those 7 dreadful days out of every month
Should be a celebration
A painful, yet beautiful reminder
That WE are the successors of creation
And the heaven sent instrument between your thighs
Is merely a portal that gives tomorrow permission to exist
Although, sometimes it cries
For the number of deaths it conceives
Because although we bring you in this world
We never truly wish to see you leave
We never look forward to that knock on the door
From anyone in uniform
Whether it be navy blue or green

There aren't enough medals or badges
To cure an unbearable sadness
Yet the darkness in our eyes
Allows for another sunrise
We maintain a smile
As we go through tribulations and trials
With no judge and no jury
We are our only defendant
Because we have inherited independence
Every day is our self proclaimed holiday
No need for permission or asking
We let the earth spin on its axis
We are the eighth wonder of the world
The unsolved mystery
If there was no her
There'd be no HIStory

Not the Furniture Store

I never liked my name
I'm not sure if it's the name itself
Or the way I sound saying it
But I love the way it looks in cursive
The way the capital "I" takes a different form
It transforms
I like the way my name is short and sweet
And unforgettable
To be imprinted on minds and hearts forever
I often say "My mother knew what she was doing when she named me"
Despite how ridiculous it sounded when she told me how she decided on it
"One day I was flipping through the Ikea catalog while pregnant with you and my water broke"
I thought it was ridiculous at first, like thank god it wasn't Target
Or that she had decided on Chinese food to satisfy a craving and had the menu in hand
But then, I began to view it differently
I thought, "That's actually powerful"
Like I had chose my own name
Like I had claimed my identity and demanded to make it known
So there's no one to blame for my having to endure
The inevitable stupidity that comes along with a name like Ikea
Upon introduction, I waste no time beating you to the punch by saying
"Yes, like the furniture store"
Do not ask me if anything is on sale this week or if you can get a discount

Don't ask me why your order hasn't been delivered yet or why it takes so long
Don't ask me why the furniture is so difficult to assemble
And don't, DO NOT ask me if I'm Swedish
I remember my 7th grade math teacher
She called me "furniture store" the entire school year
And by then my skin was pretty thick
So I took no offense nor was I embarrassed
I understood nicknames to be a form of endearment
And accepted it as such
People often ask if my name means something
After several Google searches
It turns out the dyslexic founder created the acronym for coding purposes
So in other words, it's meaningless
But I, personified, am meaningful
I am a force to be reckoned with
I am short and sweet and unforgettable
Like the letters of my name
I am to be imprinted on minds and hearts forever
I am furniture that was assembled piece by piece
With an instruction manual that makes no sense
But I still managed to put myself together
I am the epitome of DIY
I am very reasonable and aesthetically pleasing
I am not for sale
And my worth cannot be discounted
You can track me all day
But there's no telling when I'll arrive
My name is not ordinary
Like an Ashley or a Tiffany
And no offense to Ashley and Tiffany
But how many Ikea's do you know?

My mother knew what she was doing when she named me
She prophesied my destiny
So that everyone will know that I was here
And you will never forget me

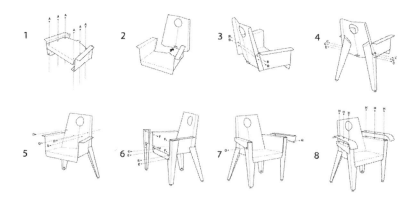

Black Angel

I won't pretend like at one point I wasn't mad at you
Like I wasn't angry at your absence
Or that I wish I were never born
Because honestly, I was mad
Angry even
A lullaby of "How could you" rocked me to sleep every night
As the tears streaming down my face saturated my pillow case
I almost hated you
Convinced myself that I should
Because I had wounds before I even exited your womb
5 counts of premeditated abandonment and I was 6th
As soon as I was old enough
My siblings wasted no time
Cordially inviting me to stand in the ashes at the stake
Where that had burned you with their words
And made sure everyone heard
My 7 year old naïve
Forced me to believe that I too should strike a match
And let the flames be a symbolism of my pain
But then something changed
Our brief, infrequent encounters began to fill in the gaps of the time lapse
But I refrained from questions like "Why did you leave?"
All I've ever known was because of drugs
A touchy subject most don't want to speak of
Only to realize that deep down

You were deprived of love
We all have demons
We all make mistakes
But I can assure you
I have accident forgiveness like Allstate
I will not continue to punish you for things you probably haven't forgiven yourself for
I will not be that constant reminder
That's there's no rewind button
I am not in a position to judge
I never got that degree
But if we are all made in God's image
Then you are one of his children
And you deserve a second chance
Because I'm sure there are a million reasons why it didn't work out the first time
I'm sure the first time you were no pro
But you weighed them against the cons
You thought you were doing what was right
So you left
Becoming someone's mother at the tender age of 14
I wouldn't expect you to have it down pact
Learning to change your pad and changing a diaper
Wasn't exactly the lesson you imagined you'd learn
At the entry of adolescence
Formula or new shoes
Diapers or a new hairdo
The potty or the party
Hearing babies scream
Battling low self esteem
Being a mom or going to prom
You were a baby having babies

And all they could seem to do was shame and place blame
But you can't point a finger without 4 pointing back
So my palms are open
And my arms spread wide
And there's nothing but unconditional love inside
You call me Black Angel
And I didn't understand why
I've never been placed on a pedestal so high
It wasn't so much the title, but the position
I was given this task to have this be different
To have this story end different
It's been passed on to me
To cut the dead limbs of this family tree
And turn over a new leaf
And start over with a new belief
Like Angels being black
I would've never imagined that
But you made me believe
In things I couldn't see
And that's all the mother
I'll ever need

2 P's no Pod

I find myself
Waiting for the right moment
To create
Instead of creating the right moment
To write
Nothing sounds the way I'd like
On paper
So I keep it in my head
Instead
And then it keeps me up at night
As I lay in bed
As I lie bed
I lie in bed telling myself I'll do it tomorrow
Knowing damn well tomorrow is more like
Next week
"I'm not in the mood" I'd say
"I don't have the urge"
"I don't feel like it"
"I don't have anything deep to say"
"I don't have anything worth talking about"
Meanwhile, time is passing me by
As tomorrow arrives
Greeting me by my bedside
With arms folded, pierced lips and a foot tap
A bath robe and a granny cap

Telling me to get my ass up out that bed
And get my day started
I carry on through my day as
The crumbs of my dreams
Leave
A trail behind me
Reminding me
That I. AM. POETRY
I inhale sonnets
And exhale soliloquies
I play with words
Nouns and verbs
And take punctuation personal
It is the imperfection
Of my perfectionism
I even scribble neatly
Still, I do not write
Even if it keeps me up at night
Because I'm wrestling demons
And procrastination is the biggest one
The ring leader of the pack
The Alpha Dog
Perfection is his right hand man
Goddamn if they ain't
A dangerous pair
For over 10 years
I let them
Tag team my dreams
Bruise my ego
Rob me of my confidence
Break our bond
And silence my voice

All this time
I've been trying to find the light
Not knowing it wasn't dark
It was just dim
And the fire has been steady burning
From deep within
I reclaim
My permissible freedom
The one that's left my knees aching
And feet calloused
From chasing a dream
While wide awake
The oxymoron alone
Leaves me exhausted
Poetry is my oxygen
And I've been on life support
For far too long
So tell the family to pull the plug
I can breathe on my own

Red Sharpie

When I was younger
My grandmother would tell me that I talk too much
It was confirmed by a red permanent marker
Decorating several pages of
My homework notebook
written sincerely by my kindergarten teacher
Stating that "Ikea is a brilliant student
but she's a little chatty"
My grandmother delivered a stern,
Hand on hip,
Finger shaking talking to
Followed by a quick yet firm smack on the mouth
I lost my 2 front teeth that night
That the tooth fairy has yet to compensate me for
From that day forth
The letters stopped
And in each class I excelled
Always at the top
Honor roll certificates covered my walls
Next to student of the month and perfect attendance
In my mind, this was excellence
showing versus telling
My actions spoke louder than my words
Because my words
Were only permissible

Of 150 characters or less
Including punctuation and indentation
Those letters home to my grandmother
Robbed me of my voice
And 50 cents under my pillow
I saved a bunch of breath from talking
By switching to writing
Because there was no punishment
For penmanship
In fact,
If there was a backhand slap responsible
For every page of every book ever written
ACS would have to get involved
But because I was only 5
Two missing teeth was a milestone
So let us not fret about the
Childhood experiences
Burned into our memories
And be grateful that they shape who we are today
Or at least that's what "they say"
I grew up knowing not to speak
Unless spoken to
And when I speak
Only say what's necessary
I have been perceived as
"Real chill" and "laid back"
But I'd beg to differ and say
I'm just well trained
And that's just the way
Things are supposed to be
I stood out from the pack
Like a red sharpie

In a pack of assorted colors
I'd pick that one first
And found reasons to use it
Maybe draw, write
Or underline
the underlying areas of my character
My kindergarten teacher
Forgot to out...line
If life still required letters home to my grandmother
I'd tell the teacher not to forget to write that
"Ikea is a brilliant student
"But she's a little chatty BECAUSE
she has a lot of great things to say
like how she can recite the entire alphabet in English and Spanish,
both harmonically
Or how she talks
because she's speaking for the other students
who haven't found their voice yet,
or because she is very capable of effectively communicating her wants and needs
so she'll have no trouble navigating this world
or maybe it's because she likes the sound of her voice
and will become a motivational public speaker or
because
she simply fucking can!
So for all those kindergarten teachers that send letters home
If you have nothing good to say
Pick a different colored sharpie

Popped Cherry

I'd like to tell you the story
About the night I lost my virginity
It was exactly how I had imagined
Ever since I was a little girl
I had played out the whole scene
Of how it would happen
I entered the room
And almost immediately my energy shifted
Even though I had planned on doing it
I still didn't know If I would follow through
But at that very moment
When she said my name
I knew it was time
I had to do it
Everyone that I admired and respected had done so already
So why shouldn't I ?
I got closer and closer
Hands trembling
Heart about to beat out of My chest
And my stomach was doing somersaults
I knew it was now or never
I had never done this before
What if I did something wrong?
What If I said the wrong things?
Would I be satisfying?

There was no way of telling
Unless I took the first step
And I did
Up the three short steps
That led to the stage
Approached the microphone
Felt the spotlight spill across my forehead
Greeted the crowd
And recited my first poem
Or at least that's how I imagined it would happen
What really happened when my name was called
Was me popping out of my seat
Like a Jack-In-The-Box
And walked toward the stage with spaghetti legs
My heart was beating so hard
I could feel it in my ears
And I was sure, certain that
Even the crowd could hear it
But almost immediately afterwards,
My heart fell silent
Like the crying baby
Who after several different rationales
Of what could be wrong has ran through your mind
You discover, all she wanted was to be held close
So that she could go to sleep
My heart has been yelling, screaming
So loud it keeps me up at night
This was the moment I had been waiting for
The moment that had been waiting for me
It was everything I thought it would be
And more
A high that you can't buy

I left feeling alive that night
And boy was I glad I came

Ode to My City

The place where subway rats
Are bigger than alley cats
And there's no such thing as rush hour
Because at every hour
Everyone is in a rush
Like, it could be 2.a.m.
Just the two of us
And you'd still push past me
To get to a seat
On an empty train!
The home of the richest poor's
Sounds like quite the oxymoron
But the average homeless person
Earns tax payer's dollars
Tax free
Around the clock
And not once did they clock in
The scent of incense and halal food
Lets me know I'm in Harlem
Where good vibes
And food that will make a toilet my bitch
Can be found
Where culture was born
And still resides
In bean pies,

Raw Shea butter and black soap
So our skin don't crack
Like the sidewalk cracks
Or the crack on the sidewalk
The place where
The winters are mean
Like the stale facial expressions of
Well…
Everyone!
And the summers are as miserable
As the old lady raising her 5 grandkids
In the 2 bedroom apartment
On the 6th floor of the building
Where the elevator doesn't work
And hotter than
The inner thighs
Of the lost 15 year old girl
Looking for love
In all the wrong places
The city where
Real musician and rawest of talent
Accompanies you on train platforms
And follows you through each car on the E train
Where fruit snacks, batteries and DVD's can all be purchased
From the comfort of your seat
Next to the girl
Who has applied so much makeup
She's now 3 shades lighter
And the kid rapping out loud to his music
That not even he understands
Or performing his latest routine
With hand claps and foot taps

Letting everyone know
"It's show time ladies and gentleman"
And the guy sitting across from you picking his nose
And then touching the pole
The city where bumper cars is played daily
On the LIE, BQE Holland and Lincoln tunnels
And the Van Wyck is a parking lot
The city where pedestrians
Have suicidal tendencies
And are color blind
Because green indeed means go…for the cars
But there's a red hand
Telling them not to walk
But defiance takes them by the hand
And invites you to walk in front of the car
Of the driver who has extreme road rage
The city where every borough
Has that local deli
That stays open 24 hours
To satisfy that 3 a.m. craving
For a chopped cheese
Or bacon egg and cheese on a roll
With 2 loosies
And a small coffee
And some even have a walk up window!
The city where parties that start at 9
Really means 11
And the Saturday night club goers
Are the Sunday morning worshippers
Where Times Square is filled with a sea of people
All
The

Time

And the bright lights are really the only main attraction

Other than the man who can paint you

A personal Mona Lisa

Or sell you chargers, umbrellas and knock off purses

The city where most of its inhabitants

Have yet to visit the landmarks that tourists travel from all over the world to see

The city that is taken for granted

The best damn city on the planet

The place that is of no comparison to another

The big apple, where everyone wants a bite.

Acknowledgments

"We were all born alone and we're all going to die alone" is a phrase I learned when I was younger and recited often. Whoever coined the phrase forgot to mention the in between part: living. As much as we like to think that we walk alone or can make it through life without any help from anyone, we are 100% incorrect. Someone, somewhere at some point has made it possible for you to be where you are today, no matter how big or small their contribution. So, I'd like to thank you Paula Sow for being a powerful leader and inspiration, Robin Devonish (the guru of self publishing) for your guidance, Michael Geffner of The Inspired Word for providing the platform for artists to share their work, Ta-Shana Taylor for recognizing my potential from day one and keeping me on the path of success, Mr. Cohen for your tough love, Alex Tatis for standing in your light and shining some my way, LT88 (Great 88!), Kurell and Ernest, Debbie, my Safespace family: Sal, Cassildra, Tamika (Ms. J), my Safe Haven family, Mack for being a paternal figure, Jennifer, Jimmy, Ms. Lydia, Mr. Moore, Ms. Dana, Ms. Rose, Shivani, Carlton, Shauna, Sabrina, JoJo, Shawn Brown, Diana Williams, Camille Singleton, Jennifer Campbell, Kimberly (Umpa), Cassandra Nady, ShaQuia and Evelyn Robinson. None of this would be possible without you!

Please send your questions, comments or concerns to contact@ikeawilliams.com